FRUITS OF
Truth

FRUITS OF TRUTH

© 1997: Christian Art
P O Box 1599
Vereeniging
1930
South Africa

Compiled by Lizette Jonker
Designed by: Christian Art

Scripture quotations are taken from the HOLY BIBLE, NEW INTERNATIONAL VERSION. Copyright © 1973, 1978, 1984 by International Bible Society. Used with permission of Zondervan Publishing House.

ISBN 1-86852-148-6

© All rights reserved. Written permission must be secured from the publisher to use or reproduce any part of this book, except for brief quotations in critical reviews or articles.

Printed in Singapore

Truth stands the test of time; lies are soon exposed.
~ King Solomon in Proverbs 12:19 ~

*Truth is the only merit that gives
dignity and worth to history.*
~ Lord Acton ~

*Truth is the secret of eloquence and of virtue, the basis of
moral authority; it is the highest summit of art and of life.*
~ Henri-Frederic Amiel ~

A half truth is a whole lie.
~ Yiddish Proverb ~

And Jesus prayed this prayer:
"O Father, Lord of heaven and earth, thank you for hiding the truth from those who think themselves so wise, and for revealing it to little children. Yes, Father, for it pleased you to do it this way!"
~ Matthew 11:25 ~

A good man is known by his truthfulness;
a false man by deceit and lies.
~ Proverbs 12:17 ~

To be and remain true to oneself and others is to possess the noblest attribute of the greatest talents.
~ Johann Wolfgang von Goethe ~

But, my dearest Agathon, it is truth which you cannot contradict; you can without difficulty contradict Socrates.
~ Socrates ~

Remember, too, that knowing what is right to do and then not doing it is sin.
~ James 4:17 ~

I have found the paradox that if I love until it hurts, then there is no hurt, but only more love.
~ Mother Teresa ~

No man ever became great or good except through many and great mistakes.
~ William Gladstone ~

He that is discontented in one place will seldom be content in another.
~ Aesop ~

He who loves money shall never have enough ... The more you have, the more you spend, right up to the limits of your income, so what is the advantage of wealth —except perhaps to watch it as it runs through your fingers!
~ Ecclesiastes 5:10-11 ~

Truth often suffers more by the heat of its defenders than from the arguments of its opposers.
~ William Penn ~

If you tell the truth, you don't have to remember anything.
~ Mark Twain ~

We believe men who witness in our courts, and so surely we can believe whatever God declares. And God declares that Jesus is his Son. All who believe this know in their hearts that it is true.
~ 1 John 5:9-10 ~

*Advice is seldom welcome; and those who
want it the most always like it the least.*
~ Lord Chesterfield ~

*The hero of my tale - whom I love with all the power
of my soul, whom I have tried to portray in all his beauty,
who has been, is, and will be beautiful - is Truth.*
~ Leo Tolstoy ~

By a lie, a man ... annihilates his dignity as a man.
~ Immanuel Kant ~

*The foundation of morality is to
have done, once and for all, with lying.*
~ Thomas Henry Huxley ~

Lies will get any man into trouble, but honesty is its own defense. Telling the truth gives a man great satisfaction.
~ Proverbs 12:13-14 ~

The first step to greatness is to be honest.
~ Samuel Johnson ~

The first and the last thing that is required of genius is love of truth.
~ Johann Wolfgang von Goethe ~

'It is,' says Chadband, 'the ray of rays, the sun of suns, the moon of moons, the star of stars. It is the light of Terewth'.
~ Charles Dickens ~

It is one thing to show a man that he is in error, and another to put him in possession of truth.
~ John Locke ~

The Jewish leaders said: "You aren't even fifty years old - and you've seen Abraham?" Jesus replied: "The absolute truth is that I was in existence before Abraham was ever born!"
~ John 8:57-58 ~

Truth exists; only lies are invented.
~ Georges Braque ~

Truth is the cry of all, but the game of the few.
~ George Berkeley ~

Trouthe is the hyeste thyng that man may kepe.
~ Geoffrey Chaucer ~

Truth is the most valuable thing we have. Let us economize it.
~ Mark Twain ~

Truth, like a torch, the more it's shook it shines.
~ Sir William Hamilton ~

Truth is the trial of itself,
And needs no other touch;
And purer than the
purest gold,
Refine it ne'er
so much.
~ Ben Jonson ~

*So absolutely good is truth,
truth never hurts the teller.*
~ Robert Browning ~

To hide hatred is to be a liar ...
~ Proverbs 10:18 ~

*Ring out false pride in place and blood,
The civic slander and the spite;
Ring in the love of truth and right,
Ring in the common love of good.*
~ Alfred, Lord Tennyson ~

Jesus said to them, "You are truly my disciples if you live as I tell you to, and you will know the truth, and the truth will set you free."
~ John 8:31-32 ~

It is easier for a camel to go through the eye of a needle than for a rich man to enter the Kingdom of God.
~ Mark 10:25 ~

For rigorous teachers seized my youth,
And purged its faith, and trimmed its fire,
Showed me the high, white star of Truth,
There bade me gaze, and there aspire.
~ Matthew Arnold ~

And who is the greatest liar? The one who says that Jesus is not Christ.
~ 1 John 2:22 ~

The truth which makes men free is for the most part the truth which men prefer not to hear.
~ Herbert Agar ~

The wicked man is doomed by his own sins; they are ropes that catch and hold him. He shall die because he will not listen to the truth.
~ King David in Proverbs 5:22-23 ~

Is not prayer a study of truth, a sally of the soul into the unfound infinite? No man ever prayed heartily without learning something.
~ Ralph Waldo Emerson ~

That a lie which is all a lie may
be met and fought with outright,
But a lie which is part the truth is a harder matter to fight.
~ Alfred, Lord Tennyson ~

Let's tell them the truth, that
there is no gains without pains.
~ Adlai Stevenson ~

If you wait for perfect conditions,
you will never get anything done.
~ Ecclesiastes 11:4 ~

I don't know what I may seem to the world, but as to myself, I seem to have been only like a boy playing on the sea-shore and diverting myself in now and then finding a smoother pebble or a prettier shell than ordinary, whilst the great ocean of truth lay all undiscovered before me.
~ Sir Isaac Newton ~

The ideals that have lighted my way and, time after time, have given me new courage to face life cheerfully have been Kindness, Beauty, and Truth.
~ Albert Einstein ~

If you want truth to go round the world you must hire an express train to pull it; but if you want a lie to go round the world, it will fly; it is as light as a feather, and a breath will carry it. It is well said in the old proverb, 'a lie will go round the world while truth is pulling its boots on'.
~ C.H. Spurgeon ~

But when you consider the wonderful truth of the prophets' words, then the light will dawn in your souls and Christ the Morning Star will shine in your hearts. For no prophecy recorded in Scripture was ever thought up by the prophet himself. It was the Holy Spirit within these godly men who gave them true messages from God.
~ 1 Peter 1:19-21 ~

A witness who tells the truth saves good men from being sentenced to death, but a false witness is a traitor.
~ Proverbs 14:25 ~

Truth fears no trial.
~ Thomas Fuller ~

Slander, meanest spawn of Hell.
~ Alfred, Lord Tennyson ~

If a man will begin with certainties, he shall nd in doubts; but if he will be content to begin with doubts, he shall end in certainties.
~ Francis Bacon ~

For great is truth, and shall prevail.
~ Thomas Brooks ~

Since the truth is in our hearts forever, God the Father and Jesus Christ his Son will bless us with great mercy and much peace, and with truth and love.
~ 2 John 1:2-3 ~

Justice is truth in action.
~ Benjamin Disraeli ~

*An unreliable messenger can cause a lot of trouble.
Reliable communication permits progress.*
~ Proverbs 13:17 ~

*I detest the man who hides one thing in the
depth of his heart and speaks forth another.*
~ Homer ~

> Truth is often a terrible weapon of aggression. It is possible to lie, and even to murder, for the truth.
> ~ Alfred Adler ~

> There is nothing which we receive with so much reluctance as advice.
> ~ Joseph Addison ~

> 'Tis strange what a man may do, and a woman yet think him an angel.
> ~ William Makepeace Thackeray ~

To be the greatest, be a servant.
~ Matthew 23:11 ~

Men are generally more careful of the breed
of their horses and dogs than of their children.
~ William Penn ~

There is no more lovely, friendly, and charming relation-
ship, communion, or company than a good marriage.
~ Martin Luther ~

Marriage has many pains, but celibacy has no pleasures.
~ Samuel Johnson ~

What can be added to the happiness of a man who is in health, out of debt, and has a clear conscience?
~ Adam Smith ~

In everything, satiety closely
follows the greatest pleasures.
~ Marcus Tullius Cicero ~

Truth is the warrant of the word,
That yields a scent so sweet,
And gives a power to faith to tread
All falsehood under feet.
~ Ben Jonson ~

This is the message God has given us to pass on to you: that God is Light and in him is no darkness at all. So if we say we are his friends, but go on living in spiritual darkness and sin, we are lying.
~ 1 John 1:5-6 ~

In this world there are only two tragedies. One is not getting what one wants, and the other is getting it.
~ Oscar Wilde ~

*A wise man is hungry for truth,
while the mocker feeds on trash.*
~ Proverbs 15:14 ~

*First, I want to remind you that in the last days
there will come scoffers who will do every wrong
they can think of, and laugh at the truth.
This will be their line of argument: "So Jesus promised to
come back, did he? Then where is he? He'll never come!
Why, as far back as anyone can remember everything has
remained exactly as it was since the first day of creation."*
~ 2 Peter 3:3-4 ~

Blessed be the name of God forever and ever, for he alone has all wisdom and all power. World events are under his control. He removes kings and sets others on their thrones. He gives wise men their wisdom, and scholars their intelligence. He reveals profound mysteries beyond man's understanding. He knows all hidden things, for he is light; and darkness is no obstacle to him.
~ Daniel 2:20-22 ~

For there are six things the Lord hates - no, seven:
Haughtiness
Lying
Murdering
Plotting evil
Eagerness to do wrong
A false witness
Sowing discord among brothers.
~ Proverbs 6:16-19 ~

Any story sounds true until someone tells the other side and sets the record straight.
~ Proverbs 18:17 ~

One may sometimes tell a lie, but the grimace that accompanies it tells the truth.
~ Friedrich Wilhelm Nietzsche ~

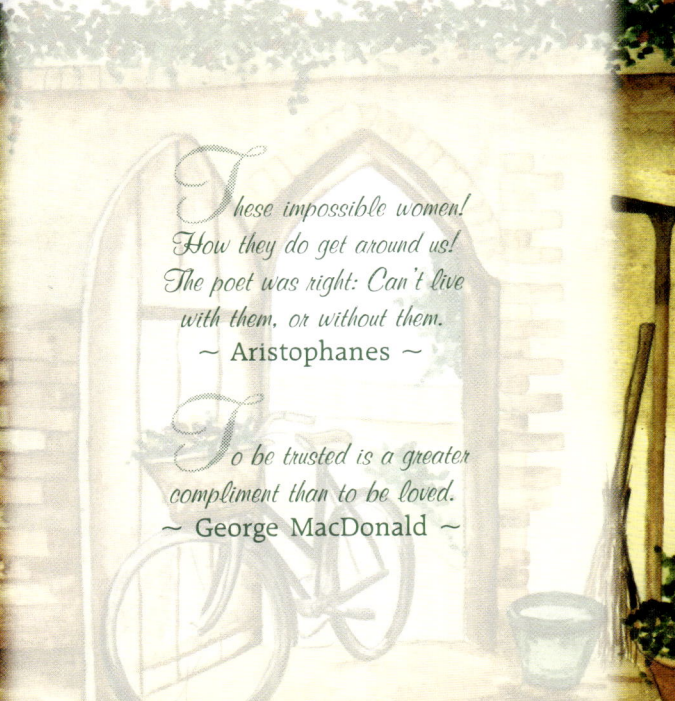

These impossible women! How they do get around us! The poet was right: Can't live with them, or without them.
~ Aristophanes ~

To be trusted is a greater compliment than to be loved.
~ George MacDonald ~

I like to walk about among the beautiful things that adorn the world; but private wealth I should decline, or any sort of personal possessions, because they would take away my liberty.
~ George Santayana ~

My beloved friends, stay true to the Lord.
~ Philippians 4:1 ~

I believe love produces a certain flowering of the whole personality which nothing else can achieve.
~ Ivan Sergeevich Turgenev ~

Jesus told him, "I am the Way — yes,
and the Truth and the Life. No one can
get to the Father except by means of me."
~ John 14:6 ~

Everything has been entrusted to me by my Father. Only
the Father knows the Son, and the Father is known only
by the Son and by those to whom the Son reveals him.
~ Matthew 11:27 ~

"And I came to bring truth to the world.
All who love the truth are my followers."
"What is truth?" Pilate exclaimed.
Then he went out again to the people and told
them, "He is not guilty of any crime."
~ John 18:37-38 ~

Fix your thoughts on what is true and good and right. Think about things that are pure and lovely, and dwell on the fine, good things in others.
~ Philippians 4:8 ~

Who may climb the mountain of the Lord and enter where he lives? Who may stand before the Lord? Only those with pure hands and hearts, who do not practise dishonesty and lying.
~ Psalm 24:3-4 ~

I do myself a greater injury in lying than I do him of whom I tell a lie.
~ Michel Eyquem de Montaigne ~

A man apt to promise is apt to forget.
~ Thomas Fuller ~

The truth doesn't hurt unless it ought to.
~ B.C. Forbes ~

There is nothing so powerful as truth — and often nothing so strange.
~ Daniel Webster ~

Sometimes the kindest thing you can do for a person is to tell him a truth that will prove very painful. But in so doing, you may have saved him from serious harm or even greater pain. In a world such as ours, people must learn to "take it". A painless world is not necessarily a good world.
~ Sylvanus and Evenlyn Duvall ~

$\mathcal{F}$*rom the cowardice that shrinks from new truth*
From the laziness that is content with half-truths,
From the arrogance that thinks it knows all truth,
O, God of Truth, deliver us.
~ Prayer of the Scholar ~

$\mathcal{S}$*ilence: the unbearable repartee.*
~ G.K. Chesterton ~

*You'll never get mixed up if you simply tell the truth.
Then you don't have to remember what you have
said, and you never forget what you have said.*
~ Sam Rayburn ~

*If you're going to tell people the truth,
make them laugh, or they'll kill you!*
~ Billy Wilder ~

*Never try to tell everything you know.
It may take too short a time.*
~ Norman Ford ~

The most powerful single thing you can do to
have influence over others is to smile at them.
~ Author Unknown ~

The world tolerates conceit from those who
are successful, but not from anybody else.
~ John Blake ~

If a man has good manners and is not afraid of
other people, he will get by even if he is stupid.
~ Sir David Eccles~

I can live for two months on a good compliment.
~ Mark Twain ~

*Think twice before you speak,
and then say it to yourself.*
~ Elbert Hubbard ~

*Truth is tough. It will not break, like a bubble,
at a touch; nay, you may kick it about all day, like a
football, and it will be round and full at evening.*
~ Oliver Wendell Holmes Jr. ~